Flip the Flaps

Farm Animals

Karen Wallace and Nicki Palin

KINGFISHER

NEW YORK

KINGFISHER
LONDON & NEW YORK

Copyright © Kingfisher 2009
Published in the United States by Kingfisher,
175 Fifth Ave., New York, NY 10010
Kingfisher is an imprint of Macmillan Children's Books, London.
All rights reserved.

Consultant: David Burnie

First published in hardback in 2009 by Kingfisher
This edition published in 2012 by Kingfisher

Distributed in the U.S. and Canada by Macmillan,
175 Fifth Ave., New York, NY 10010

Library of Congress Cataloging-in-Publication data has been applied for.

ISBN: 978-0-7534-6738-1

Kingfisher books are available for special promotions and premiums. For details contact:
Special Markets Department, Macmillan, 175 Fifth Ave., New York, NY 10010.

For more information, please visit www.kingfisherbooks.com

Printed in China
3 5 7 9 8 6 4 2
2TR/1212/UNTD/LFA/128MA

Contents

Sheep

Many different animals live on a farm. Sheep live outside in the fields all year round, eating grass. Their woolly coats keep them warm. The farmer brings the sheep inside only when they have lambs.

shearing (cutting off) a sheep's coat

sheep in a field

4

1. A fleece is a sheep's woolly coat. It can be made into wool.

2. Some farmers paint spots on their sheep so that they can find them if the sheep get lost on another farm.

sheepdog

3. A sheepdog runs around to help the farmer move the sheep.

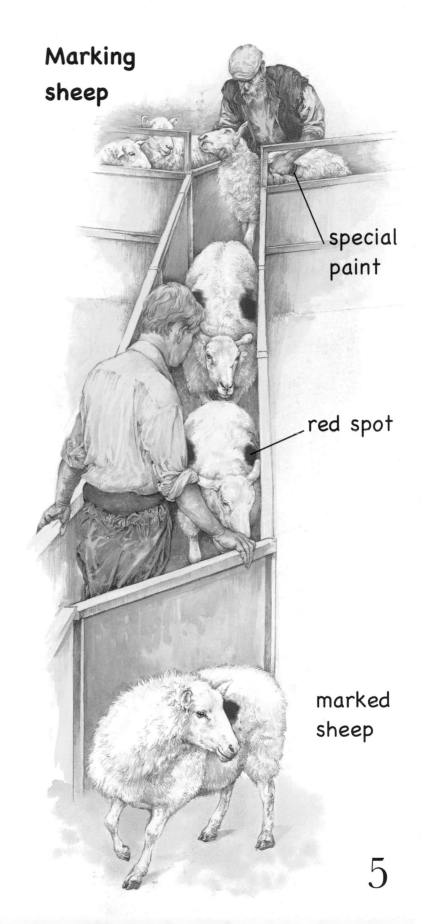

Marking sheep

special paint

red spot

marked sheep

5

Pigs

There are many types of pigs. Some pigs are huge and spotted. Others are brown or black and white. Most farmers keep large, pink pigs because they have a lot of piglets and produce good meat.

pig warming up
in the sunshine

mother pig
sleeping

6

1. A pig rolls in mud to stay cool and protect its skin from the sun.

2. Pigs eat a mash made out of barley and wheat. They also like cabbages and other vegetables.

3. A mother pig has around eight to eleven piglets.

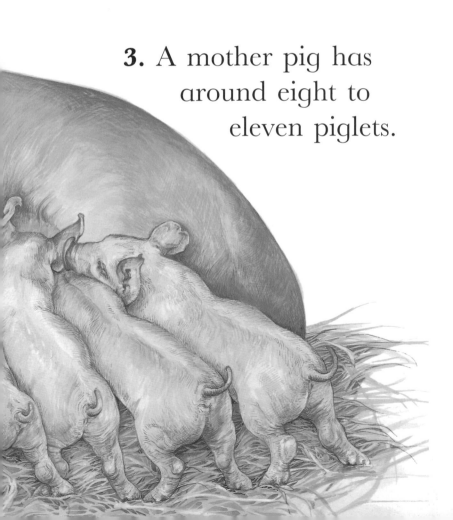

Pigs eating . . .

mash from a feeder

vegetables from a trough

cabbage from a bucket

Goats

Goats do not like being alone, so they stay together in a group, called a herd. Most farmers keep goats for their milk, which they make into cheese.

herd of goats in the mountains

**kid
(a baby goat)**

horn

beard

two male billy goats

1. Some goats graze in the mountains in the summer. In the winter, they move down to the farm.

2. Goats like plants to eat and space to play. They also like to sleep.

Goats enjoy . . .

eating

3. Goats use their horns to butt each other when they are fighting.

playing

sleeping

Chickens

At night chickens sleep
in a special house to keep
them safe from wild animals.
In the morning the rooster
wakes them up with a
loud cock-a-doodle-doo!

chicken scratching
the ground

rooster
(a male chicken)

10

1. A chicken scratches the ground with her feet to find insects and worms to eat.

2. Chickens can have short or long, fluffy or spotted feathers. Roosters have long tail feathers.

3. A mother hen sits on her nest to keep her eggs warm and help them hatch.

Some types of feathers

fluffy feathers

spotted feathers

rooster

long tail feathers

11

Cows

Many farms are home to a large herd of cows. In the summer, the cows live outside in the fields and eat grass. Baby cows, called calves, live with the herd.

herd of cows eating grass

calf drinking its mother's milk

12

1. In the winter, cows eat hay and grain. They live inside a shed.

2. Farmers keep cows for their meat (beef) and milk. Milk can be made into cheese, yogurt, and butter.

3. A farmer uses a milking machine. It has special tubes to suck out the cow's milk.

using a milking machine

Some foods from cows

beef pie

roast beef

hamburger

milk

cheese

yogurt

butter

13

Horses

On some farms, horses pull carts or help plow fields, but on most farms, horses do not work. The farmer and his or her family enjoy taking care of the horses and riding them across the fields.

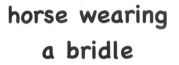

horse wearing a bridle

bridle

tools for
taking care of
the horse's hooves

14

1. A bridle is a set of leather straps for a horse's head. It helps control the horse.

2. Yes. There are big and small horses, spotted horses, and racehorses, which gallop very fast.

3. A horse wears metal horseshoes to stop its hooves from wearing down.

horseshoe

Some types of horses

Shire horse

Shetland pony

Appaloosa

racehorse

Ducks

Most farmyard ducks have white feathers and orange beaks. Mallard ducks, which are wild, are different colors. They visit farms to build a nest beside a river or pond.

cleaning feathers with beak

male duck

female duck

mallard ducks swimming in a pond

webbed foot

1. A duck cleans its feathers to stop them from soaking up water when it swims. Then it shakes out old feathers.

Ducklings hatching

Ducklings grow inside eggs . . .

2. Ducklings hatch after they have grown inside an egg for one month.

and then the eggs hatch.

3. Ducks have webbed feet to help them paddle around and dive underwater.

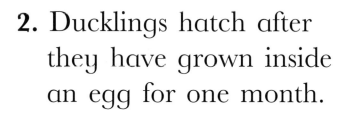

nibbling plants at the bottom of the pond

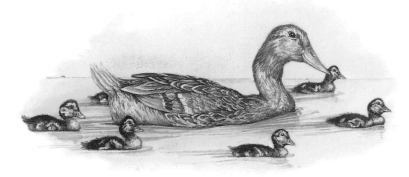

The ducklings soon learn to swim.

17

Index